New Light On The
GAUGE CONVERSION

by

C. R. Clinker

CONTENTS

AN AVON-ANGLIA PRODUCTION

Avon-AngliA Publications & Services,
9 Poplar Avenue, Bristol BS9 2BE

ISBN 0 905466 12 8

INTRODUCTION

It is not easy to picture the railway network of Great Britain in 1845 when the great decision was about to be taken whether the country's railways should be standardised on one gauge and, if so, what that gauge should be. The country was divided by companies, the Great Western and its associates providing the Broad Gauge (7ft) main line from London to Bristol and Exeter with branches Didcot to Oxford and Swindon to Gloucester, a total of only 246 miles against some 1,900 of Narrow Gauge (4ft 8½in) belonging to the rest of the companies. The Eastern Counties and Northern & Eastern had converted from a 5ft gauge to Narrow Gauge in September 1844; and the 32-miles Dundee & Arbroath and Arbroath & Forfar already agreed to change over from 5ft 6in to Narrow Gauge.

Not only was there established Broad Gauge mileage, but a further 658 was proposed in plans deposited at the Board of Trade, to which were added 63 miles actually authorised in 1844. Whilst the inconvenience of break of gauge, actual or potential, at certain junction stations was admitted on all hands, the Great Western party had no intention of giving up the operating advantages claimed for their Broad Gauge. The matter was discussed in Parliament and, on the motion of Cobden in the Commons, a Royal Commission was appointed to enquire whether future Acts should provide for securing a uniform gauge and whether it would be practicable to bring existing lines, and those in process of construction, within such uniformity.

The Broad Gauge companies pressed their case strongly before the Commission but in the end lost the day. Considering that two out of the three Commissioners had attained distinction in the academic world only, and that Sir Frederic Smith alone possessed any practical experience of railway working, the report is characterised by a remarkable breadth of view and appreciation of the actual difficulties of the subject. The Bill passed into law on 18 August 1846 as 'An Act for Regulating the Gauge of Railways'. It prohibited construction of railways in Great Britain on other than the Narrow Gauge (in Ireland 5ft 3in) except in connection with existing Broad Gauge lines, those wholly south of the Great Western main line or in the four western counties, viz: Cornwall, Devon, Somerset and Dorset. Thus, apart from the onus placed on promoters to prove before Parliament the necessity for laying the Broad Gauge on their railway, little progress was made towards attaining uniformity of gauge.

So, construction of lines on the Broad Gauge went ahead, 1,232 miles being laid in the 31 years between the passing of the Act and opening of the St. Ives branch on 1 June 1877. These 4¼ miles, apart from a few chains in the Plymouth harbour area in 1879, were the last Broad Gauge section brought into use. But five years earlier the first large scale conversion to Narrow Gauge had been carried out in South Wales.

Padstow, Cornwall.
January 1978.

C. R. CLINKER

Broad, Mixed and Narrow Gauge Lines West of Exeter, May 1892

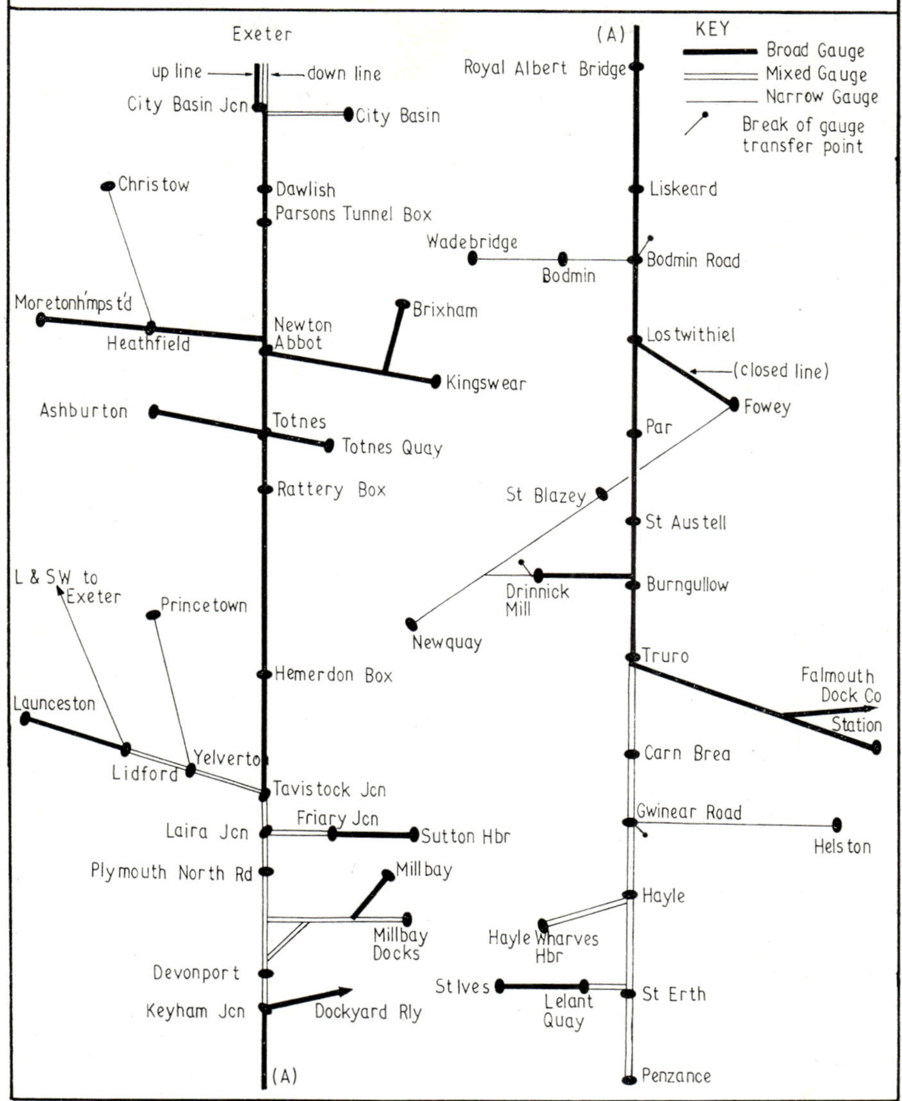

GREAT WESTERN RAILWAY.

ALTERATION OF GAUGE

OF THE

MAIN LINE

BETWEEN

EXETER & TRURO,

AND OF THE FOLLOWING

BRANCH LINES

BETWEEN

NEWTON ABBOT	and	MORETONHAMPSTEAD.
NEWTON ABBOT	„	KINGSWEAR.
CHURSTON	„	BRIXHAM.
TOTNES	„	ASHBURTON.
TAVISTOCK	„	LAUNCESTON.
TRURO	„	FALMOUTH.
ST. ERTH	„	ST. IVES.

NOTICE IS HEREBY GIVEN,

That the lines of the Company between the above-mentioned points will be altered from the Broad to the Narrow Gauge, commencing on the night of Friday, May 20th, 1892.

During the time the alteration is being made the lines specified will be closed and all traffic upon them entirely suspended until the work is completed, which is expected to be on the night of Sunday, May 22nd.

THE FRONT COVER OF THE GWR PUBLIC NOTICE COVERING THE CONVERSION FROM BROAD TO NARROW GAUGE (*C. R. CLINKER*)

New Light on the Great Western Railway
Gauge Conversion, 1892

Something of the engineering and operating feat in carrying out final abolition of the Broad Gauge on the Great Western Railway in 1892 is well known to many students of railway history, but very little has appeared in print about the actual organisation of this work, the preliminary discussions at all levels, the mass of contingent details which had to be worked out, and so on. It is the purpose of this booklet to throw some light on these lesser known aspects, though to treat them fully in every detail would require a considerable volume, so much source material having come to hand in recent years.

When the GWR Board decided on 29 October 1835 to adopt Brunel's recommendation that their new line should be laid on the seven-feet, or Broad Gauge, they can hardly have realised the heavy expenditure which would fall on the company in the years ahead, or the bitterness and antagonism which would result. Friction with other companies, complaints from the public—especially about conditions at Gloucester—were rife as early as 1845. Barely a year later the subject was raised in Parliament and a Royal Commission appointed, consisting of Sir Frederic Smith, Lieutenant-Colonel in the Royal Engineers, George Biddell Airy, quaintly described as 'Astronomical Observator' (Astronomer Royal) at Greenwich Observatory, and Peter Barlow, Professor of Mathematics at Woolwich Military Academy. When the Commission's report was issued there were 246 miles of Broad Gauge and just over 1,900 miles of Narrow Gauge in use. Though on balance the evidence given to the Commissioners shewed the superiority of the Broad Gauge on most counts, their report recommended standardisation on the Narrow Gauge and, it is sometimes forgotten, conversion of all Broad Gauge lines to Narrow Gauge. The Regulation of Railway Gauges Act 1846 prohibited, with certain defined exceptions, construction of further Broad Gauge mileage beyond that already sanctioned or under construction. It did not make conversion compulsory, nor was there ever any legislation on this aspect.

Mixed Gauge—that is Broad and Narrow combined, with a common rail (except in a few special cases)—was first laid in 1847 between Gloucester and Cheltenham to accommodate Great Western trains on the existing Birmingham & Gloucester Company's Narrow Gauge route. It is interesting to notice that this section was laid on transverse sleepers, not on Brunel's longitudinal baulks. Mixed Gauge was subsequently employed wherever a Narrow Gauge company ran over GW metals, as at Bristol, where it became convenient to work through vehicles from Narrow to Broad and vice versa.

Mainly for financial reasons the GWR, which had a somewhat unusual agreement-cum-lease with the South Wales Railway—a Broad Gauge system of 175 miles stretching from Grange Court, just west of Gloucester, to New Milford (Neyland)—resisted the call of the South Wales coal owners to convert to

Narrow Gauge and so eliminate the damage and consequent loss caused by transfer at Gloucester and elsewhere. But the red—or perhaps one should say the yellow—light had been seen at Paddington. The inconvenience caused by lack of through working with other lines and consequent necessary transhipment eventually forced the Board to a reluctant realisation that they were in a minority and would remain so. At the end of 1865 the company owned 598 miles of Broad Gauge, 236 miles of Mixed and 416 miles of Narrow, a total of 1,250 miles. The conversion of the South Wales main line and connecting branches in 1872, followed by the Wilts, Somerset and Weymouth section (Chippenham to Salisbury and Westbury to Weymouth and branches) two years later, along with sundry other lines, actually reduced the Broad Gauge figure to 8 miles by April 1875. In the following year the Bristol & Exeter and South Devon Companies were amalgamated with the Great Western and the working of the Cornwall Railway taken over, bringing the Broad Gauge total up to 327 miles; the Mixed mileage (including the jointly-owned West Cornwall) was 219 and the Narrow 1,421 miles. Thereafter the Broad Gauge figure declined steadily as conversions continued until, at the end of 1891, only 171 miles remained, 42 double and 129 single. With the exception of the Taunton - Chard branch (where Broad Gauge was retained to counter London & South Western Railway attempts to obtain running powers), the whole mileage was west of Exeter. The Cornwall Railway also was pressing for abolition of the Broad Gauge, but after receiving a lengthy report from the General Manager, Grierson, the Board decided against making a change on financial grounds.

However, five years later the subject came up again in a somewhat better financial climate, although other factors had now to be taken into account. In order that the final abolition of the Broad Gauge might be considered, the Board called for a detailed report shewing the whole of the works which would have to be carried out by all departments, the cost, and the savings which would accrue from conversion. This lengthy and informative document, dated 2 February 1891, was drawn up by the General Manager, Henry Lambert. On 26 February a meeting attended by Frederick G. Saunders (Chairman), Viscount Cobham (Deputy Chairman) and the company's chief and divisional officers recommended that the final conversion should take place in May 1892.

At their meeting on 5 March 1891, the GW Board discussed the relative merits of doing the work in 1892 or 1893. Because the quadrupling of the line between Taplow and Didcot and doubling on the South Devon between Rattery and Hemerdon at a total cost of £700,000 was already in hand, any further heavy commitments were thought unwise. No definite decision was taken until the meeting on 19 March when, on Lambert's advice, the Board agreed to the gauge conversion taking place in May 1892, by a vote of 14 for, 2 against.

A sub-committee—'The Gauge Committee' consisting of directors and officers, in itself a rather unusually democratic body for the times, was set up to organise this tremendous engineering and operating programme, with all its mass of detail which had to be taken into account.

On the recommendation of the Gauge Committee the Chard branch—the only entirely Broad Gauge line between Bristol and Exeter—was agreed to be converted on 18 - 20 July 1891 and all lines Exeter to Penzance and branches over the weekend between the night of Friday 20 May and the early morning of Monday 23 May, 1892. The Gauge Committee set to work at once to organise the conversion of the whole of the remaining Broad Gauge lines to Narrow Gauge, together with the necessary ancillary works in sidings and locomotive depots, conversion of locomotives and rolling stock or provision of new units, alterations to traders' privately-owned wagons, structural alterations at stations, strengthening of bridges, etc.

As if this was not a sufficient task, the Board of Trade had, under the Reguation of Railways Act 1889, issued an Order to the company on 20 November 1890 requiring installation of interlocking apparatus and new signalling west of Exeter, the abolition and replacement by bridges of nine level crossings on the West Cornwall section below Truro, and replacement of the rather primitive telegraph and crossing-order method of signalling by full block telegraph on double lines and electric train staff on single lines. This was to be the first use of the electric staff on the Great Western system, between Dawlish and Parsons Tunnel, in October 1891. A study of the record of staff misdoings shews the somewhat primitive state of the signalling west of Exeter, especially the absence of interlocking—which allowed points to be moved whilst vehicles were passing over them—and reliance entirely on telegraph, with 'crossing orders' to prevent two trains meeting head on in single line sections west of Plymouth, as they had done on several occasions.

The Down 'Dutchman', headed by locomotive *Eupatoria*, passes 'Twyford, Junction For Henley' at speed on 14 May 1892 (*British Railways*)

Broad gauge train near Exminster in May 1891 (*Author's Collection*).

In all, this massive programme was estimated to cost between £2½ and £3 million pounds spread over two years. Because of the difficulty in differentiating between works which were treated as integral parts of the gauge conversion and those carried out at the same time as a matter of convenience and/or economy, it is impossible to calculate precisely how the expenditure should be allocated. Neither the recorded estimates nor the actual expenditure, in fact, answer the question. The cost was lumped together in one sum, apart from the essential division into capital account and revenue account. Lambert's report is largely made up of statistics—mileages and costs. To make for easier understanding, the relevant portions are reproduced on pages 24 - 27.

Before the actual conversion is considered, there are some contingent matters to record. The Board of Trade's Order relating to signalling etc., required completion within three years. The Signal Engineer and the Telegraph Superintendent estimated the signalling and interlocking would cost £81,600 plus £92,641 for new wires, apparatus, removal of poles etc., and £2,057 per year for additional staff at places between Exeter, Falmouth and Penzance. If the West Cornwall line was to be kept open at night, an additional £800 per year would be needed. The further requirement of the Order that nine level crossings west of Truro must be replaced by bridges would cost about £19,250, but if retained they could be gated and signalled for £500 each, including the provision of a cottage as stipulated.

Various other companies and bodies were concerned in the gauge conversion. Among these were the London & South Western Railway at Chard and the third rail on its line between Exeter and Crediton (over which the Great Western exercised the former Bristol & Exeter company's running powers), the Narrow Gauge Teign Valley at Heathfield and the Cornwall Minerals Railway at Par, at both of which places direct junctions could be made. The Admiralty's Keyham branch, leading to a system within the Dockyard, and the Falmouth Dock Company's private railway were also involved. The owners of 46 private sidings had also to be consulted and agreed with.

Lambert's report calculated a balance of loss of £19,641 arising out of the gauge conversion itself and carrying out the works in connection therewith, although the present author has found it impossible to determine just how this figure was arrived at. However, against this there were considerable advantages to be weighed, viz:

"(a) of 78 miles of present single line between Devonport and Penzance, 54 miles will be double

(b) stations will be so substantially enlarged and improved that very few new works of any importance will be required west of Bristol for many years to come

(c) new locomotive establishments will be provided at Truro, Newton Abbot and Taunton

(d) the line will be worked by Block Telegraph and interlocked in accordance with Board of Trade requirements

(e) three timber viaducts—Milltown, Tregarne and Tregagle—will be reconstructed in stone."

Lambert added that conversion would give fresh impetus to passenger and goods traffic and he confidently expected that the necessary additional traffic (£40,000 per annum or £770 per week) would be forthcoming.

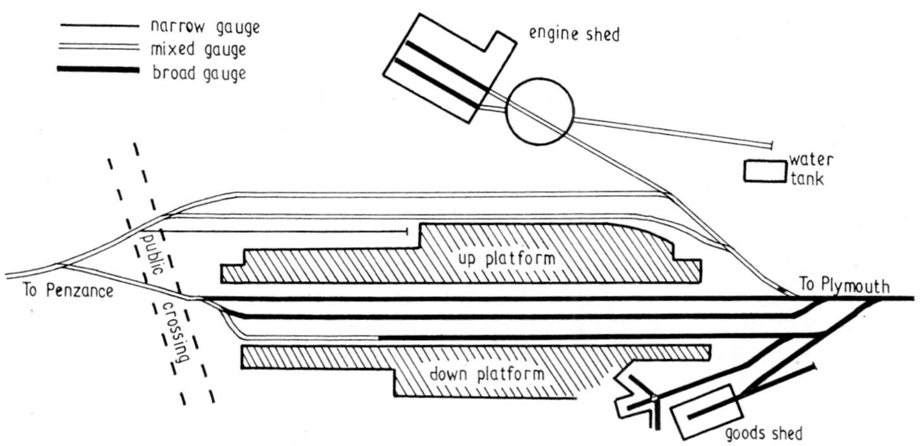

PLAN OF TRURO JOINT STATION (CORNWALL AND WEST CORNWALL RAILWAYS), MAY 1859. H.S. BUSH, ENGINEER

On 10 February 1892 the Gauge Committee considered a lengthy report from the Chief Engineer, Louis Trench, newly-appointed from the strongly anti-Broad Gauge London & North Western Company. He estimated 2,900 men would be needed for conversion of running lines and 1,200 to deal with the station yards. The Plymouth Engineering Division would furnish about 1,300 men and the remainder (2,800) would be drawn from the Taunton, Reading, Neath, Hereford, Wolverhampton and Newport Engineering Divisions. A further 300 - 400 to handle work in the locomotive sheds would be provided by the Locomotive and Carriage Department. In the event, the total was 4,700 men, including 52 inspectors; the Plymouth Division supplied 1,300 many of whom were, of course, on their 'home ground'.

The men would be divided into gangs of 60 under an inspector and three gangers. Superintendence of the work was to be delegated to two Divisional Engineers—Hammet to cover Exeter to Plymouth and branches, and Gibbons part of his normal area between Plymouth and Penzance with the branches. The whole operation was to be under the control of the Chief Engineer in person.

The men would provide their own food for the weekend, the company supplying cooking appliances, also oatmeal and boiling water for the men's use. Each man to receive an allowance of 25 per cent in addition to his regular wages during the period of conversion, plus 1/- (5p) extra for each night away from home.

For sleeping accommodation goods sheds, station waiting rooms etc., would be used; tents to accommodate 63 men at 23 sites in country areas and the hiring of two lofts, one at Coryton and one at Lifton (near Launceston), would also be necessary. A tender from Messrs John Edgington was recommended for acceptance:—

2/- (10p) per man for tent accommodation
6d (2½p) per man for waterproof ground sheet
8d (3½p) per man for sleeping bags
2/- (10p) per man for horse rugs

The total cost was about £500. The whole of Trench's proposals were subsequently approved by the Board and took place as proposed.

The Gauge Committee next considered the traffic working arrangements proposed by N. J. Burlinson, Superintendent of the Line. These fell into several categories and it will be convenient to treat them as having taken place as proposed. There were no changes of any importance.

1. Every Broad Gauge goods vehicle west of Exeter, including private owners' wagons and those on outlying sidings and private lines, e.g. Teignmouth and Totnes Quays, Keyham Dockyard and the Falmouth Dock Company's lines, had to be worked away. A general restriction on acceptance of all goods and mineral traffic, after 7 May, for stations west of Exter was imposed to allow time for transit and clearance. Commencing on 16 May, special trains conveyed these to Swindon for conversion or scrap; a few were taken to Lostwithiel, Newton Abbot and Bridgwater shops for conversion, these being the former Cornwall, South Devon and Bristol & Exeter wagon works respectively.

10.15 A.M. TRAIN FROM PADDINGTON, FRIDAY, MAY 20TH.

37. On Friday, May 20th, the 10.15 a.m. Train from Paddington will call at several additional Stations, and the following are the times at which the Train will work:—

		arr. a.m.	dep. a.m.	
	Paddington	—	**10 15**	
	Swindon	**11 42**	**11 52**	
	Bath	**12 30**	**12 35**	
	Bristol	**12 53**	**1 0**	
	Taunton	**1 51**	**1 55**	
	Exeter	**2 34**	**2 42**	
	Dawlish	**3 0**	**3 2**	
	Teignmouth	**3 9**	**3 11**	
	Newton Abbot	**3 20**	**•3 25**	**• Precede 9.0 a.m. ex Paddington.**
	Brent		3 56	
	Kingsbridge Road		4 1	
	Ivybridge		4 6	
	Hemerdon		4 11	
	North Road	**4 25**	**4 26**	
	Ticket Platform	**4 29**	**4 32**	
	Plymouth (Mill Bay)	**4 33**	**4 45**	
	Devonport	**4 50**	**4 52**	
	Saltash	**4 59** X	**5 0**	X **4 50 p.m. Passenger ex Saltash.**
	St. Germans	**5 10**	**5 11**	
	Menheniot	**5 24** X	**5 25**	X **2.0 p.m. Passenger ex Penzance.**
	Liskeard	**5 33**	**5 34**	
	Doublebois	**5 42**	**5 43**	
	Bodmin Road	**5 53**	**5 55**	
A	**Bodmin Road**	—	**6 0**	
A	**Bodmin**	**6 10**	**7 24**	
A	**Boscarne Junction**	—	**7 30**	
A	**Wadebridge**	**7 42**	—	
	Lostwithiel	**6 2**	**6 4**	
	Par	**6 15**	**6 17**	
B	**Par**	—	**6 20**	
B	**St. Blazey**	**6 22** X	**6 25**	X **5.30 p.m. Passenger ex Newquay.**
B	**St. Blazey**	—	**6 26**	
B	**Fowey**	**6 37**	—	
B	**Bridges**		6 X 31	X **5 20 p.m. Mineral ex St. Dennis Junction.**
B	**Bugle**	**6 39**	**6 40**	
B	**Victoria**	**6 45**	**6 46**	
B	**St. Column Road**	**6 57**	**6 59**	
B	**Newquay**	**7 12**	—	
	St. Austell	**6 29** X	**6 32**	X **5.0 p.m. Passenger ex Penzance.**
	Burngullow	**6 37**	**6 38**	
	Grampound Road	**6 47**	**6 48**	
	Ticket Platform	**7 1**	**7 4**	
	Truro	**7 5**	**7 10**	
Special.	**Truro**	—	**7 22**	**The 8 5 p.m. from Truro to Falmouth in connection with the 6.25 p.m. ex Penzance will not be run on May 20th.**
Special.	**Perranwell**	**7 29**	**7 30**	
Special.	**Penryn**	**7 38**	**7 40**	
Special.	**Ticket Platform**	**7 47**	**7 49**	
Special.	**Falmouth**	**7 50**	—	
	Chacewater	**7 21**	**7 22**	
	Scorrier Gate	**7 27**	**7 28**	
	Redruth	**7 33** X	**7 35**	X **6 25 p.m. Passenger ex Penzance.**
	Carn Brea	**7 39**	**7 40**	
	Camborne	**7 44**	X**7 46**	X **7.0 p.m. Train of Empties.**
	Gwinear Road	**7 51**	**7 53**	
	Hayle	**8 0**	**8 1**	
	St. Erth	**8 5**	**8 7**	
C Special	**St. Erth**	—	**8 25**	
C Special	**Carbis Bay**	**8 27**	**8 28**	
C Special	**Lelant**	**8 35**	**8 36**	
C Special	**St. Ives**	**8 40**	—	
	Marazion Road	**8 14** X	**8 15**	X **8.5 p.m. Passenger ex Penzance.**
	Penzance	**8 20**	—	

NOTE.—Bristol Tickets must be collected at Bath, Taunton Tickets at Bristol, and Exeter Tickets at Taunton. Passengers in the 9.0 a.m. Train from Paddington for Stations beyond Plymouth should be transferred into the 10.15 a.m. Train at Newton Abbot.

A The 5.10 p.m. Train from Bodmin Road to Bodmin will leave at 4.40 p.m. off the 2.0 p.m. Train from Penzance, leaving Bodmin at 5.24 p.m. (present time) for Wadebridge. The 6.2 p.m. Train from Bodmin to Bodmin Road will leave at 5.45 p.m., and the 6.25 p.m. Train from Bodmin Road to Bodmin will leave at 6.0 p.m. to connect with altered 10.15 a.m. Train.

B This Train will run in place of the 5.35 p.m. Par to Newquay and Fowey, which will not run on May 20th.

C This Train will run in place of 8.50 p.m. St. Erth to St. Ives, which will not run on May 20th.

FROM PENZANCE

FRIDAY, MAY 20th.

Last Broad Gauge Train.

PENZANCE TO SWINDON.

	arr. p.m.	dep. p.m.
Penzance		9 10
Marazion Road	9 15	9 17
St. Erth	9 25	9 26
Hayle	9 30	9 32
Gwinear Road	9 40	9 42
Camborne	9 48	9 50
Carn Brea	9 54	9 55
Redruth	10 0	10 2
Scorrier Gate	10 8	10 9
Chasewater	10 13	10 15
Truro	10 25	10 33
Grampound Road	10 48	10 50
Burngullow	10 59	11 0
St. Austell	11 5	11 7
Par	11 15	11 17
Lostwithiel	11 27	11 29
Bodmin Road	11 36	11 38
Doublebois	11 53	11 55
Liskeard SATURDAY MORNING	12 3	12 5
Menheniot	12 13	12 15
St. Germans	12 26	12 28
Saltash	12 40	12 42
Devonport	12 49	12 52
Plymouth Mill Bay	1 0	1 10
Plymouth North Road	1 13	1 17
Mutley	1 18	1 21
Plympton	1 28	1 30
Cornwood	1 43	1 45
Ivybridge	1 50	1 53
Kingsbridge Road	2 0	2 3
Brent	2 8	2 10
Totnes	2 16	2 18
Newton Abbot	2 47	2 57
Teignmouth	3 7	3 9
Dawlish	3 16	3 20
Starcross	3 28	3 31
Exminster	3 39	3 42
St. Thomas	3 50	3 54
Exeter	4 0	4 10
Taunton	5 25	5 45
Bridgwater	6 15	6 25
Highbridge	6 40	6 50
Bristol	7 55	8 5
Bath	pass	8 32
Chippenham	9 2	9 10
Swindon F Cabin	9 45	a.m.

"F" Cabin Swindon will be open continuously from 6.0 a.m. Monday, May 16th, until 6.0 p.m. Saturday, May 21st.

FROM STATIONS EAST OF EXETER (INCLUSIVE).

All Broad Gauge Stock from Stations on this Section of the Line must be worked to Swindon as quickly as possible after **May 17th**, and on Friday and Saturday, May 20th and 21st, **SPECIAL TRAINS** with empty stock must be run to Swindon as required. The Superintendents will make the necessary arrangements for doing this.

Reproduced on *page 11* is the timetable of the last through Broad Gauge train from Paddington, pictured on the front cover; *above* is the Up working from Penzance to Swindon.

(*Above*) A Broad Gauge 4-2-2 heads an Up train through the old station at Flax Bourton. Note the Mixed Gauge crossover in the foreground; (*below*) an 1890 six-coach Up train of very mixed stock leaves the double line to enter the single line section over Ivybridge timber viaduct. *Author's Collection* (*L&GRP*)

2. Similarly, but in a much shorter period, all passenger coaches—which were stripped of lamps, label boards, spare screw couplings etc. before despatch—were worked to Swindon on Friday evening, 20 May, in fourteen special trains from Penzance, St Erth, Truro, Liskeard, Plymouth and Newton Abbot. The last Broad Gauge train west of Exeter was the 9.10 p.m. empty coaches from Penzance which left Exeter at 4.10 a.m. on the Saturday morning for Swindon.

3. On the same day—Friday 20 May—the Narrow Gauge coaches and other stock required to form the first trains on Monday 23 May were worked down to Plymouth via the London & South Western route from Exeter. There was little difficulty in providing stock at Penzance, Truro and Falmouth as this could be supplied from the Cornwall Minerals Railway depot at St Blazey (which was wholly Narrow Gauge) and from Carn Brea, the West Cornwall Railway depot, that company being equipped with Mixed Gauge on which nearly normal services were run. The Teign Valley, Princetown, Bodmin, Wadebridge, Fowey, Newquay and Helston branches had always been Narrow Gauge and suitable passenger and goods services were maintained on them during their temporary 'isolation'.

4. Meantime, starting on Thursday 19 May, special trains bringing the army of workmen from all over the system were setting out for Exeter, where there was still a break of gauge and those not arriving in Broad Gauge stock had to change. One compartment in every four was retained and labelled for the men's tools, the owners travelling in the three adjoining compartments. The routing of these trains—there were fourteen in all—was so arranged as to provide a service from nearly all Great Western stations. A good example was the one from Chester to Exeter via Shrewsbury, the Severn Valley, Worcester Foregate Street (picking up a contingent from stations between Honeybourne and Worcester), Ledbury—where a connecting special train from Chipping Norton Junction (now Kingham) via Cheltenham was waiting—Severn Tunnel, Bristol (for some men from Swindon to join) and so to Exeter, taking just twelve hours. It carried 440 men and their tools and personal effects.

5. Having brought the men down, the coaches had to be stabled. On Friday 20 May all the Broad Gauge stock was worked to Swindon for scrap, and the Narrow Gauge to sidings at Weston-super-Mare.

6. The conversion being completed, the men were returned home on Tuesday in seven special trains—Narrow Gauge, of course—the empty coaches being worked down from Weston-super-Mare and Bristol. The last train left Exeter at 12.30 p.m. for Tondu. On both the forward and return trains the timetable provided for stops at specified mileposts between stations where there was tented accommodation for outlying gangs.

7. Although some interference with the convenience of the travelling public was inevitable, this could not be tolerated where the conveyance of mails was concerned, remembering that there was a Sunday delivery at that time. Here the London & South Western was involved. The down mail and passenger train at 9.0 p.m. from Paddington on the Saturday and Sunday of 'conversion week-

end' was run Narrow Gauge, reversed at Exeter to the South Western route and so via Lydford and down the Mixed Gauge Tavistock branch, reaching Plymouth at 4.20 a.m.

On Sunday morning the mails were taken by road to Millbay Docks and put aboard the steamer *Gazelle*, from the company's Channel Islands service, which left Plymouth at 5.20 a.m. for Fowey and Falmouth. A network of horse coaches then distributed the bags throughout Cornwall. They returned to the two ports with the Sunday despatches and the same arrangements operated in reverse. It may be of interest to add here that, despite the early start, the steamer was crowded to capacity with Plymouth people on the trip to Falmouth and back for 1/6d. (7½p). The day, as was the whole week-end, was one of perfect weather and calm sea. A touch of realism was provided by the employment of guards in uniform with the mail coaches. Horns were blown as they progressed through the countryside. Ten coaches leaving Falmouth within minutes of each other must have been a brave sight in 1892.

THE PLANS ARE EXECUTED

So much for the bare details of the more important minute arrangements necessary to the success of this tremendous engineering and operating change-over. There are numerous other features which could be mentioned—indeed, enough to fill a sizeable book. Undoubtedly it was the very great care taken to cover every contingency, even the most unlikely, right down to naming individual members of the staff and their exact responsibilities, which resulted in one hundred per cent success in carrying through the whole plan.

Broad Gauge locomotives at Swindon awaiting scrapping. *Author's Collection (L & GRP)*

Arrangements having been made to hand over to the Engineers any Broad Gauge siding or otherwise unwanted track before 'conversion week-end', a good deal of advance preparation was done. Because of exceptional difficulties in dealing with Royal Albert Bridge, this was converted on Sundays several weeks earlier by laying a separate Narrow Gauge track inside the Broad Gauge one, this being then merely connected up at each end, leaving the Broad Gauge rails to be lifted at leisure. The Engineers had also made other preparations. New points and crossings were got ready on the sites, ballast cleared out between rails, bolts oiled, transoms cut and other steps taken which would not affect the safety of the road before conversion.

To the last detail, the whole of the arrangements worked perfectly in the superb weather. On Friday 20 May the very last Broad Gauge train—the 9.10p.m. empty coaches from Penzance to Swindon, as already mentioned—called at every station as far as Exeter. At each place Inspector Scantlebury, after receiving a verbal assurance from each Station Master in person (delegation of this duty was strictly prohibited) that no Broad Gauge vehicles remained at his station or at outlying sidings under his control, handed out a certificate to him that this was the last Broad Gauge train. The certificate was passed to the Engineers and conversion started literally within minutes. Much of the work was finished ahead of time and by the Sunday afternoon nearly all was completed. In fact, conversion of all the running lines was completed in thirty one hours.

Every section was then carefully tested by the Engineers running inspection engines over the whole lengths, including crossovers and sidings, and a certificate given by the accompanying Inspector to the Station Masters. On Monday 23 May the normal train service was resumed—on the Narrow Gauge—although trains ran a few minutes late because the drivers had been instructed to keep speeds down until the track had consolidated. There was no mishap of any kind during or after the conversion; only one incident was reported, a workman taken ill at Bodmin Road and rushed to hospital in Plymouth by one of the inspecting engines. Certainly a triumph of organisation and a reminder that we today have no monopoly of such things.

A word should also be said in praise of the press. Having been given every facility to see the work in progress, accurate and very detailed accounts appeared in both local newspapers and the London dailies. Some were given permission to interview the gangers and workmen. The *Royal Cornwall Gazette* at Truro carried a very full, almost hour by hour, account of the progress of work in its area. Surprisingly, no similar official account seems to have survived. Perhaps everyone was too busy to keep a diary or log. Photographs of the work on the line are few, although the trains attracted attention, of course.

At their meeting on 2 June 1892 the Directors minuted their satisfaction that the conversion had been carried through without a hitch and commended everyone who had any part in it, from the General Manager to the workmen. A copy of this minute was distributed so as to reach all concerned.

1st September 1892.

Dear Sir,

In receiving the report of the carrying out of the conversion of the Gauge on the Co's Lines in the West of England in May last, the Board expressed themselves as highly gratified at the successful completion of the operation and at the hearty manner in which every member of the Staff engaged in it had performed his share of the work.

Thinking it may be of interest to you, I have the pleasure to send you the accompanying copy of the minute which was passed by the Directors on the occasion.

Yours faithfully,

G. K. Mills.

The letter of appreciation, headed Great Western Railway, London Terminus, Paddington.

The workmen were allowed some rest on the Monday—they had worked for seventeen hours on each of the two preceding days—before their return trains left early on the Tuesday morning. All that remained could be attended to by the local Engineering and Signal Department staffs i.e. removal of waste material, completion of minor conversions and so on. The redundant third rail between Paddington and Bristol and in the Plymouth and West Cornwall areas was removed by the end of the year (1892). All that could then be seen of Brunel's Broad Gauge in situ was on a few small wagon turntables, so popular in Victorian times. One, at Swindon, was still to be seen in 1950.

The scene opposite, top left, shows conversion in progress on the original line between Saltash and St Germans; note the shipping backdrop. The picture on the right vividly portrays activity at Forder Viaduct on the same line, closed in 1908 on the opening of the present line. The illustration bottom left shows the task in detail while the Dawlish scenes below contrast 1890 Broad Gauge with 1892 Mixed Gauge. The double track illustrates Broad Gauge cross sleeper track with Narrow Gauge chairs laid in and, on the Down Line, the Broad Gauge joint of cross sleeper and baulk roads.
Author's Collection (*L & GRP*)

The Track

It is certainly interesting, even surprising, to note that railway preservationists were around in 1892. Several letters appeared in Plymouth newspapers urging the Directors to offer one of the magnificent 'Iron Duke' class engines and a typical Broad Gauge carriage—all to be scrapped—as the nucleus of a museum at Beaumont Park. Alas nothing came of this; there is no evidence that the plea reached the Board. All we have to remind us of the Broad Gauge era so far as rolling stock is concerned (apart from a number of quite well preserved carriage bodies in use as sheds etc) is the South Devon's ridiculous little 'coffee pot' engine *Tiny* preserved on Newton Abbot station. As MacDermot remarked, 'it is to be hoped that future generations will not come to regard it as a typical broad gauge engine'.

A great deal of sentiment was poured forth at the passing of the Broad Gauge for which many people clearly had a great and genuine affection. The smooth riding at speeds well above other companies' trains and the comfortable carriages in use in 1892—they were 11ft 6ins wide, about two feet wider than today's coaches—were obviously thought of as unlikely to be reproduced on the Narrow Gauge. It is a sad thought that the unprogressive management at Paddington during the latter days of the Broad Gauge, with its fine and powerful locomotives, prevented the travelling public from really seeing what the Broad Gauge could offer in the way of high speed combined with comfort and safety. It was, perhaps, a mercy that Sir Daniel Gooch died three years before his beloved Broad Gauge was abolished, although it is a pity he could not have seen it at its best.

One personal reference concludes this section. The supply and distribution of all materials necessary to the gauge conversion was the responsibility of the Chief Storekeeper, Mr Dunn. The conversion completed, Mr Dunn, then 85 years of age, tendered his resignation. He joined the company in 1840, had been Storekeeper since 1867 and so was responsible for supplies for the 1872 South Wales conversions and two years later the Wilts, Somerset & Weymouth changeover. He was succeeded by W. H. Stanier, father of Sir William Stanier. Dunn retired to live at Teignmouth where he died in 1910 at the age of 103. What railway history he must have seen!

GREAT WESTERN RAILWAY.

"CONVERSION OF GAUGE."

This is to certify that the Line between Menheniot and Saltash is ready to be re-opened for Traffic, and the ordinary working of Trains between those points can be resumed on Monday, the 23rd.

W. H. Wright, *Traffic Inspector.*

To the Station Master St. Germans *Station.*

May 20th, 1892

Extract from
Royal Cornwall Gazette 26 May 1892

Perhaps nowhere between Exeter and Penzance was the work of narrow gauging the line more intricate and heavy than at Truro.

This was owing to the fact that the gauges were mixed and seeing that the work was accomplished with such dispatch, those who took part in the operation are to be all the more congratulated.

The whole success of the work depended upon the admirable planning and aforethought which enabled the heads of each department to know thoroughly what was expected of them.

The chief official commanding the Truro section of the employees was Mr. Smith, of the engineers' department, who acted as inspector from Carvedras viaduct to the ticket platform west of the station.

Under him were 1 ganger and 20 men from Bristol, 4 smiths and strikers, a carpenter, a mason, 11 viaduct men, 5 Truro gangers, with their staff of 8 viaduct and yard men, 11 skilled plate layers, 35 packers, and 3 cooks.

Mr. Swinney, of the locomotive department, had under him 1 chargeman, 1 fitter, 1 smith, 4 engine men, 4 carriage and waggon department men, 2 carpenters, and 12 labourers and cleaners.

In addition to these Mr. Brewer, the station master, who, throughout, managed the work of his department with great skill and courteously into the bargain, had on duty a staff consisting of 5 signal men, 3 telegraph clerks, 16 guards and brakesmen, and about 20 porters.

The majority of the latter were engaged during the progress of the work in preventing onlookers from obstructing the men, and in this they were greatly assisted by members of the police force of the city, to whom Mr. Brewer is deeply indebted for their valuable services.

The locomotive men worked in spells of 12 hours, but the engineer's men who were actually engaged in the conversion, worked on Saturday from 3 a.m. to 9 p.m., with three half-hour breaks for meals.

On Sunday they worked from 3 a.m. to 9.30 p.m. with two half hour breaks, and about a quarter of an hour during which they attended a short religious service. In addition to this the heavy work at the station required the constant attention of these men on the previous Friday from 6 a.m. to 8 p.m. with only three breaks each of half-an-hour's duration, and they continued their labours on Monday and Tuesday from 6 a.m. to 9.30 p.m., with intervals of only two half-hours each day.

This will give some idea of the laborious work which had to be accomplished, of the splendid stamina of the men who at all times seemed to be ready for any work required of them and were moreover desirous of the work being done thoroughly and well.

On Friday morning a gang of sixty men, who had arrived overnight and slept in the well of the goods shed on straw mattresses, warmly covered with thick blankets, commenced operations at four o'clock on the dock siding, which is about a quarter of a mile in length.

Within a few hours the line, from the point where it met the main to the Dock Company's land, had been altered, and attention was next turned to the centre line of rails into the station.

During the breakfast hour, which intervened, a short service was conducted amongst the men, and before resuming their labours, they heartily joined in the singing of two or three hymns.

By night everything as intimated, had been accomplished that could be done, and at 8.20, when the last of the broad gauge stock, consisting of two engines and a few carriages, were despatched to Swindon amid cheers and the firing of rockets, and the certificate transferring possession was handed over by Mr. Hocking, the station master, to the representative of the engineering department, only the main traffic line remained to be converted.

The Inspector who superintended the work in the station yard, Mr. C. N. Cox, had no fear whatever that by Sunday evening there would be no broad gauge line extant, and had hopes of completing the work perhaps twenty-four hours before.

In front of the signal box, where the points form an intricacy of rails, whole sections were bodily removed, and new rails were put together close at hand and switched into position with very little trouble.

The alteration of the gauge had also to be carried out over the dock system, which extends to somewhere about five miles of rails. For the purpose extra men have been employed, but as there is no immediate necessity to have the work done within a few hours, it will probably be spread over a week or more.

Saturday proved a heavy day for the men. They worked from three in the morning until nine at night, and accomplished by far the major portion of the conversion in the station yard.

Outside the yard the alteration of gauge was effected some hours before nightfall and everything cleared away, so that those of the public who expected on Sunday morning to see from the bridges the men working on the line beneath were surprised to discover all traces of the change so soon cleared away.

Resuming at four on Sunday morning, the gang in the yard quickly put the points in order to receive the first engine from Truro, which left about eleven, and at one o'clock everything was practically completed.

Inspector Rolf had under his charge 16 skilled men of the Reading signal locking engineer's department, and there were three clerks and two-time men ready in the telegraph department to assist in making telegraphic communications where necessity compelled a temporary dis-arrangement.

(NOTE — This portion of the extract, and part of page 23, refer to Falmouth).

The drink served out to the men consisted of oatmeal, and at first this was somewhat resented in some quarters, but we have it on good authority that after they had tasted it, it was partaken of with considerable relish and that since several of the men have expressed themselves as being able and willing to have more. This was a feather in the cap of the temperance folk, for we are informed that this liquid seems to have sustained the strength of the men and enabled them to do their work in a manner that could not have been done on intoxicating beverages.

There was accommodation for 84 men to sleep at the goods stations and in tents erected for them and everything was done for their comfort.

Notwithstanding the lateness of the hour (11.25 p.m.) when the last broad gauge train in England passed through Truro station, on Friday evening, there was a large concourse of people to witness the event and amid cheers and the explosion of fog signals the train left the station, Mr. Brewer having at 11.12 received from Inspector Scantlebury a certificate to the effect that that was the last train to travel from Penzance to Truro on the broad gauge.

At 9.55, Inspector S. Buckingham, of Truro, had similarly certified with regard to the Falmouth branch.

It was at the first break of day following this, that the men set to work with a will and a determination which resulted in the splendid success which we have to record.

Merchants thinking the work would not be completed in the time laid down by the Company made traffic very heavy by dispatching increased quantities of goods in case there should be delay, while the Mount's Bay fishermen had to receive more than ordinary accommodation at the last minute.

But the Company was true to its word for on Monday morning within a minute of the stipulated time the first narrow gauge train steamed into Truro station amid the onlook of many of the citizens.

It was on Sunday afternoon that Mr. Brewer in company with the engineer, Mr. H. Lott, ran a train over the newly laid line from Falmouth to Par for the purpose of "consolidating" the line, and after a very honest test, the train which had started from Truro at 5.23 p.m., arrived at Par at 7.46.

Here it met the train from the section above, showing the narrow gauge running line was clear through those sections, and at 11.14 p.m. that night, the final certificate was given to Mr. Brewer by Mr. Lott, though Mr. Brewer's duties did not cease until nearly 1 a.m. on Monday morning.

On Monday morning fish empties were worked to Penzance and enabled a fish train to proceed up country the same day, and traffic was conducted as usual.

Smart work was carried out by the men under Messrs. J. and P. Jenkins, who opened up the line between Truro and a mile or so west of Perranwell (six or seven miles altogether) by eight o'clock on Saturday evening when the first engine was run over it. Although the main line was completed for Monday morning's traffic, a great deal of course remains to be done even now in the sidings, and this is being proceeded with.

EXTRACTS FROM THE GENERAL MANAGER'S REPORT TO THE BOARD OF DIRECTORS DATED 2 FEBRUARY 1891

Lenth of main line[1] laid on the Mixed Gauge from which the third rail can be taken up:

	Double line		Single line	
	M.	C.	M.	C.
Paddington - Acton	3	20		
Acton - Bristol New Sidings[2]	113	40		
Bristol New Sidings - Exeter	77	27		
Bristol Harbour Line			1	00
Dunball Wharf			0	38
Bridgwater Docks			0	76
Exeter - Exeter Basin Branch Jcn.			1	25
Exeter Basin branch			0	34
Tavistock Jcn. - Marsh Mills	0	18		
Marsh Mills - Lidford			19	13
Tavistock Jcn. - Plymouth	3	55	0	12
North Road - West Jcn.[3]	0	24		
Laira Jcn. - Friary Jcn.	0	59		
Cornwall Jcn. - Devonport station	1	16		
Devonport station - Weston Mill Viaduct			1	25
Truro - Penzance			25	69
Hayle Wharves line			0	50
St Erth - Lelant			1	08
	200	19	52	30

TOTAL: 252M. 49C.

1 'Main Line' in the report refers to running lines i.e. not sidings.
2 Bristol East Depot
3 Devonport Jcn.

Rails and timbers to be removed:

Main line	455M.	5½C.	(including switches, crossings,
Sidings	69M.	49C.	guards and fixed points)

Gross value	£137,888 . 0 . 0d
Cost of removal	30,106 . 0 . 0d
Nett value	£107,782 . 0 . 0d

Reduction in maintenance cost by removal of third rail is estimated by the Engineer at £32,221 per year, an average of about £61 . 10s per mile of single rail per year. In the Plymouth Division track is now being altered from longitudinal to cross-sleeper; saving is based on the latter type.

Main lines to be converted from Broad to Narrow Gauge

	Double line		Single line	
	M.	C.	M.	C.
Chard branch			13	08
Exeter - Exeter Basin Branch Jcn.			1	25
Exeter Basin Branch Jcn. - Dawlish	10	58		
Dawlish - end of Parsons Tunnel			1	33
Parsons Tunnel - Rattery	19	72		
Newton Abbot - Moretonhampstead			12	09
Newton Abbot - Torquay	5	68		
Torquay - Kingswear			8	66
Brixham branch			2	01
Rattery - Hemerdon			11	20
Hemerdon - Tavistock Jcn.	4	34		
Lidford - Launceston			12	34
Friary Jcn. - Sutton Harbour	1	03		
Sutton Harbour - North Quay Wharves			0	32
Weston Mill Viaduct - Truro			50	78
Truro - Falmouth			11	68
Lelant - St Ives			3	14
	41	75	128	68
	TOTAL:	170M.	63C.	

The approximate cost of narrowing the gauge of main line, branches and sidings —excluding station alteration or improvements, locking, signalling or electrical apparatus—would be £99,227 made up as follows:

	£	£
London - Bristol	NIL	
Bristol and Exeter section		
Main line sidings	496	
Chard branch	2,625	3,121
South Devon section		
Main line and branches	12,148	
Strengthening viaducts and bridge floors	5,000	
Station yards and sidings	23,707	
Traders' sidings	703	41,558
Cornwall and West Cornwall sections		
Keyham Jcn - Falmouth & Lelant - St Ives	6,100	
Strengthening viaduct & bridge floors, etc.	13,500	
Station yards and sidings	10,990	
Traders' sidings	646	
Level crossing cottages	1,700 *	
Bridges in place of level crossings	19,300 *	
Land to be Purchased	2,312	54,548
	TOTAL:	99,227

* to meet Board of Trade requirements that all level crossings West of Exeter must be locked and signalled.

Saving in Transfer and Shunting expenses based upon 1889 statistics

	Transfer			Shunting		
	£	s.	d.	£	s.	d.
Didcot	105	4	10	—		
Bristol	—			826	16	0
Taunton	65	0	0	—		
Exeter	1817	15	10	2323	12	0
Heathfield	143	19	10	—		
Bodmin Road	102	3	10	—		
Par	94	7	1	—		
Truro	1	17	0	—		
Gwinear Road	50	0	0	—		
TOTALS:	2380	8	5	3150	8	0

(The large amounts at Exeter due to the Bristol & Exeter Railway being worked on the Narrow Gauge from 1876 and the South Devon on the Broad Gauge. At Didcot, Taunton, Heathfield, Bodmin Road, Par and Gwinear Road all traffic had to be transferred from Broad Gauge main line to Narrow Gauge branches.—C.R.C.)

Traders' Private Broad Gauge Wagons

These total 184, the largest owners being Sully & Co., coal merchants at Bridgwater (75) and the West of England Stone & China Clay Company, St Austell with 58, but the Solicitor's opinion is that the Company is not liable for the cost of conversion. (In the event, the G.W. Board agreed to contribute half the cost of conversion on request from some of the smaller owners, as had been done in South Wales in 1872.—C.R.C.)

Rolling Stock

	Converted BG to NG	Repaced by new NG*
	£	£
Locomotives—122 @ £120	14,640	
75 @ £1300		97,500
Coaching Stock—Carriages 376 @ £60	22,560	
54 @ £650		35,100
Vans 73 @ £40	2,920	
26 @ £250		6,500
Horse Boxes and 120 @ £30	3,600	
Carriage Trucks 72 @ £120		8,640
120 duplicate bogies for converting 8-wheel carriages		8,400
Wagons 800 @ £20	16,000	
2642 @ £60		158,520
TOTAL:	£374,380	

*each replacement allows for the value of disused Broad Gauge stock.

Swindon—14M. 66C. of temporary sidings for reception of Broad Gauge stock until converted or condemned—preparing ground, laying with second-hand material £8,500. Land required 3 acres @ £296 per acre purchased from the Rolleston Trustees. TOTAL: £9,388

Engine Sheds—altering gauge of engine pits and sidings in engine sheds and workshops at Penzance, Falmouth, Plymouth, Newton Abbot, Exeter, Bridgwater, Bristol, Swindon and Paddington estimated at £9,500. New and larger sheds required at Truro and Newton Abbot at £15,000 each and at Taunton £10,500. TOTAL: £50,000

Doubling of Lines

Rattery - Hemerdon	now in progress
Devonport station - Penzance (78 miles)	is single line

The Board of Trade will not sanction continuance of working single lines by block telegraph only, and train staff working will have to be introduced. The passenger service over the Cornwall and West Cornwall lines has increased, followed by a large increase in traffic. The through working of coaches from the North to watering places in the West of England will probably bring further increases. Break of gauge at Bristol has impeded full development and deterred many passengers from travelling. (N.B. The through coaches would be from the Midland Railway, and also via the Severn Tunnel after December 1886.)

On the Cornwall line there is already land enough for a double Narrow Gauge line, except at Royal Albert Bridge and over timber viaducts not yet rebuilt. Tunnels and overbridges—except a small 3-arch bridge between Liskeard and Doublebois—have been built for double line.

The large number of timber viaducts between Devonport and Truro not yet rebuilt (N.B. 20 out of a total of 33 were still in their 1859 form) will prevent immediate doubling. It is recommended the following portions be dealt with in the order named:

	M.	C.	Estimate £
Liskeard - St Austell (including reconstruction of Milltown Viaduct)	21	20	70,300
Burngullow - Truro Viaduct (including reconstruction of Tregarne and Tregagle Viaducts)	11	29	55,500
Truro - Chacewater	4	40	16,600
Chacewater - Camborne	7	30	32,000
St Erth - Ponsandane (Penzance)	4	60	14,600
Gwinear Road - St Erth	4	60	18,200
Additional land required			2,250
	TOTAL:		£209,450